I0824492

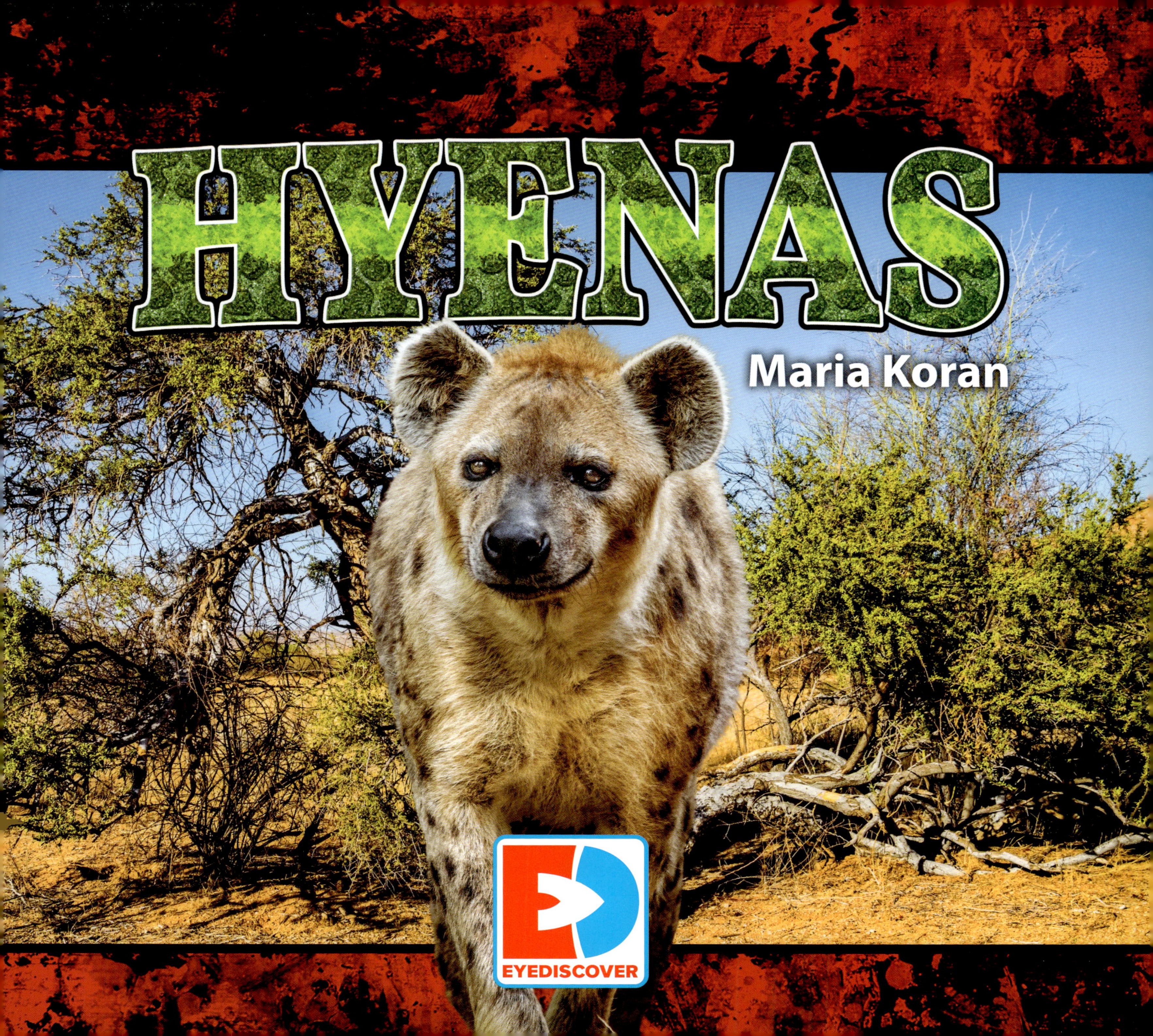
HYENAS
Maria Koran
EYEDISCOVER

Go to www.openlightbox.com and enter this book's unique code.

BOOK CODE

AVG23566

EYEDISCOVER brings you optic readalongs that support active learning.

Published by Lightbox Learning Inc.
276 5th Avenue, Suite 704 #917
New York, NY 10001
Website: www.openlightbox.com

Library of Congress Control Number: 2022935955

ISBN 978-1-7911-4875-1 (hardcover)

Printed in Guangzhou, China
2 3 4 5 6 7 8 9 0 28 27 26 25 24

022024
240209

Project Coordinator: John Willis
Layout: Sushant Deshpande

The publisher acknowledges Getty Images, Minden Pictures, and Shutterstock as the primary image suppliers for this title.

EYEDISCOVER provides enriched content, optimized for tablet use, that supplements and complements this book. EYEDISCOVER books strive to create inspired learning and engage young minds in a total learning experience.

Your EYEDISCOVER Optic Readalongs come alive with...

Audio
Listen to the entire book read aloud.

Video
High resolution videos turn each spread into an optic readalong.

OPTIMIZED FOR

- TABLETS
- WHITEBOARDS
- COMPUTERS
- AND MUCH MORE!

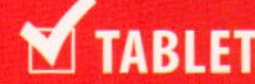

HYENAS

In this book, you will learn about

- what they are
- what they look like
- how they live

and much more!

Hyenas are animals that live in Africa and Asia. There are four types of hyenas.

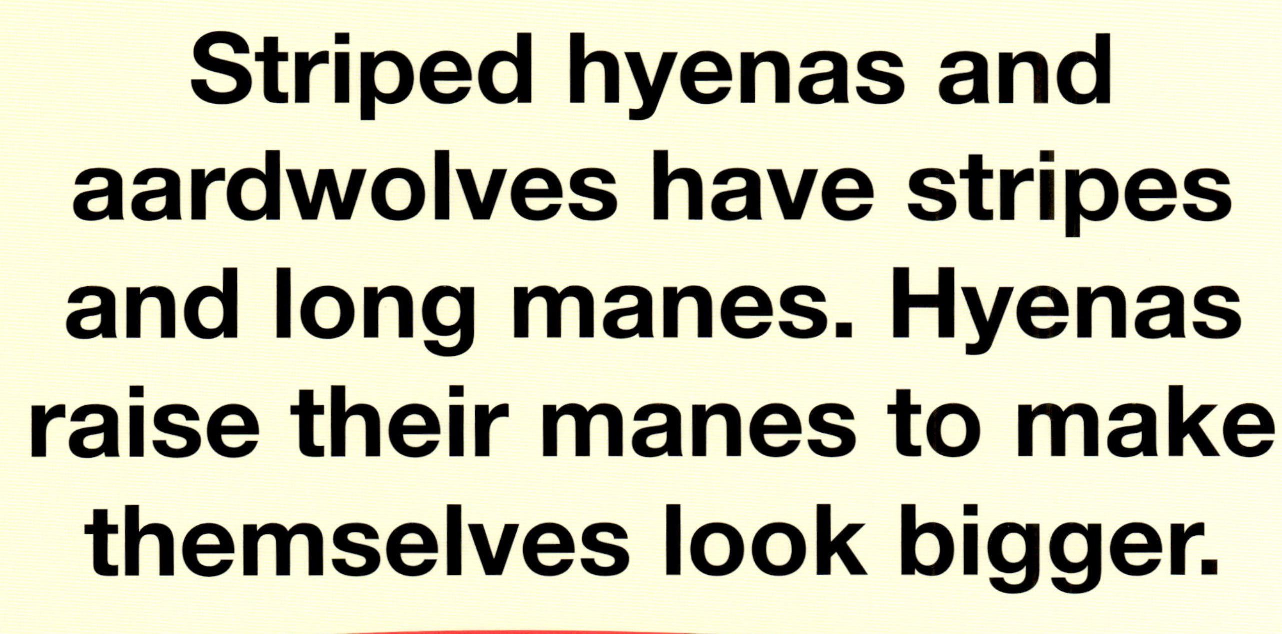

Striped hyenas and aardwolves have stripes and long manes. Hyenas raise their manes to make themselves look bigger.

Brown hyenas have long, dark hair. They can live in drier places than other hyenas.

Spotted hyenas are the largest and most well-known hyenas. They live in groups called clans.

Spotted hyenas hunt for most of their food. A clan works together to chase other animals.

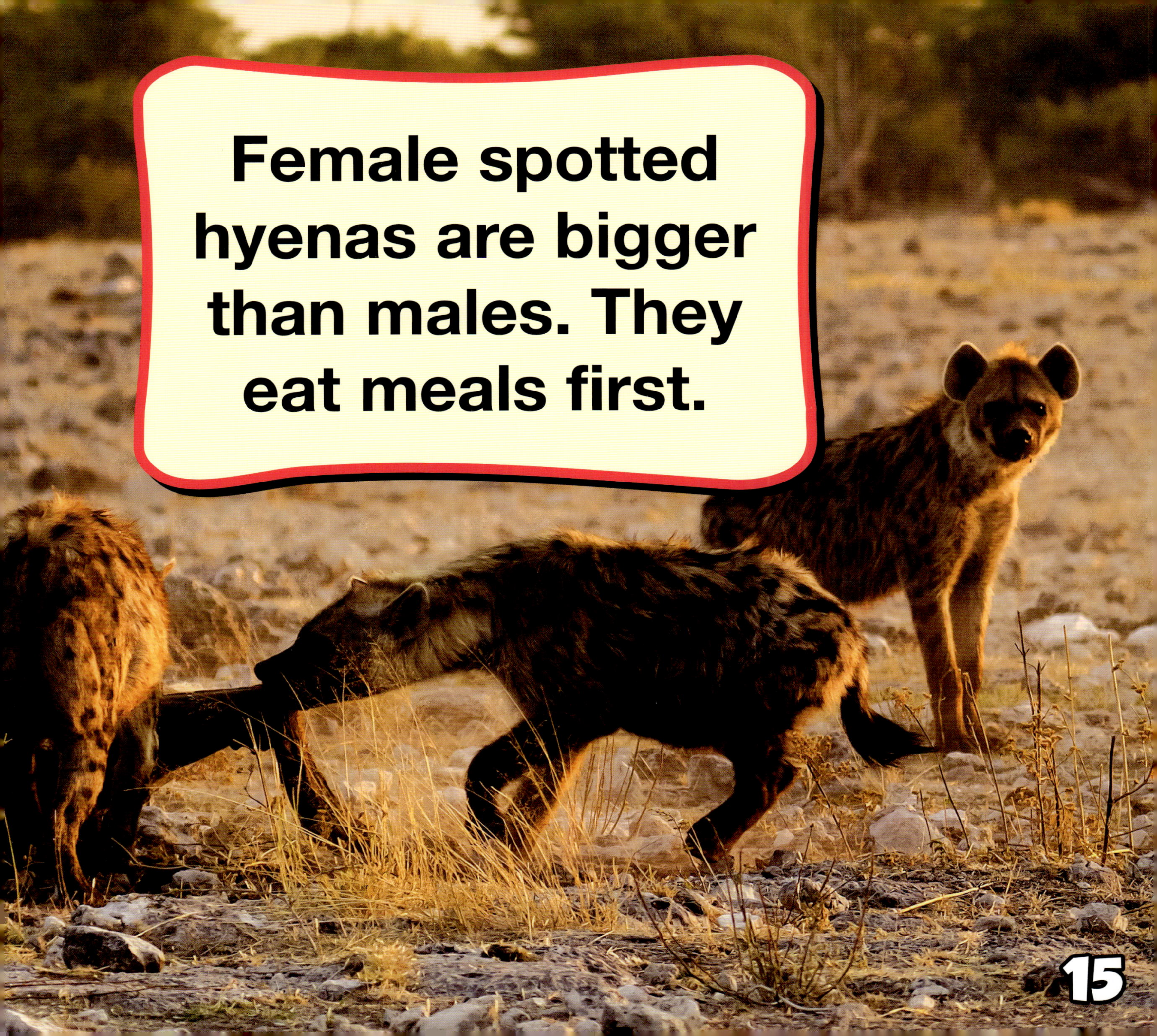

Female spotted hyenas are bigger than males. They eat meals first.

Spotted hyenas use many sounds to speak to each other. They make noises that sound like cackles, yells, and laughs.

To stay cool during the day, spotted hyenas rest in shallow holes or pools.

Young hyenas are called pups. Spotted hyena pups are born with black fur and sharp teeth.

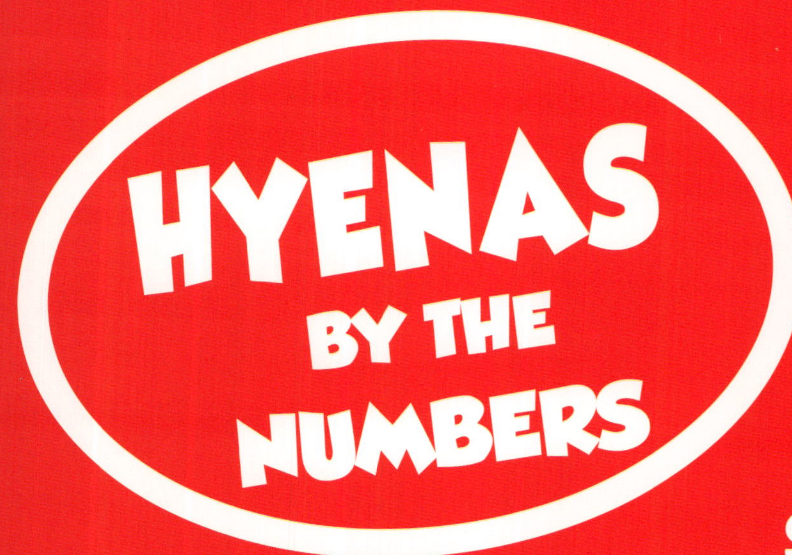

Spotted hyena clans can have more than **80 members.**

Aardwolves mostly eat **termites.** One aardwolf can eat **105 million** termites in a **year.**

A **spotted hyena** can **live** more than **20 YEARS** in nature.

Spotted hyenas can **RUN** at speeds of **37 miles** (60 kilometers) per hour.

When a **striped hyena** raises its **mane**, it can look about **40 percent larger** than normal.

Spotted hyenas can weigh more than **175 pounds** (80 kg).

KEY WORDS

Research has shown that as much as 65 percent of all written material published in English is made up of 300 words. These 300 words cannot be taught using pictures or learned by sounding them out. They must be recognized by sight. This book contains 39 common sight words to help young readers improve their reading fluency and comprehension. This book also teaches young readers several important content words, such as proper nouns. These words are paired with pictures to aid in learning and improve understanding.

Page	Sight Words First Appearance
4	and, animals, are, four, in, live, of, that, there
7	have, long, look, make, their, to
8	can, other, places, than, they
11	groups, most, the
12	a, food, for, together, works
15	eat, first
16	each, like, many, sounds, use
19	day, or
20	with, young

Page	Content Words First Appearance
4	Africa, Asia, hyenas
7	aardwolves, manes, striped hyenas, stripes
8	brown hyenas, hair
11	clans, spotted hyenas
15	males, meals
16	cackles, laughs, noises, yells
19	holes, pools
20	fur, pups, teeth

Watch
Video content brings each page to life.

Browse
Thumbnails make navigation simple.

Read
Follow along with text on the screen.

Listen
Hear each page read aloud.

Go to www.openlightbox.com and enter this book's unique code.

BOOK CODE

AVG23566